Squid Pr‹

Recipes with a Favor for the Flavor

Keith Pepperell

ISBN-13: 978-1544909677
ISBN-10: 1544909675

DEDICATION

To my spawn Jack, Lydia, and Alexandra
only one of whom is a squid person

ACKNOWLEDGMENTS

The Cisco Squid

Billy the Squid

The Crew of the Calamari Celeste

The Cincinnati Squid

Calamari Blessed Among Squid

Quimbush Merkin

Lady Estima Davenport

Muriel Dinwiddy

Squid Lovers Everywhere

Paul Asman and Jill Lenoble – Calamari Squidward

1. THE NAUGHTY SQUID

Ancient Roman kitchen help in a short tunica with seafood, including two plump squid

For thousands of years squid or calamari have been enjoyed throughout the Mediterranean although ancient recipes are not common.

Presently, squid eating had extended from the ancient world and is a global phenomenon.

Most squid rarely grow beyond a couple of feet in length, even though according to ancient folk-lore hideously enormous creatures existed. In the 13th. century Icelandic saga, Örvar-Oddr, for example, a massive creature the Kraken, over a mile long, dined on ships and their crew.

It has been reported: "According to some tales, the Kraken was so huge that its body could be mistaken for an island. This is a 13th century Icelandic saga involving two sea monsters, the Hafgufa (sea mist) and the Lyngbakr(heather-back).

The Hafgufa is likely to be a

reference to the Kraken.

 Around that time (circa 1250), another report about the Kraken was documented in a Norwegian scientific work.

 It said that only two existed because they could not reproduce and would need so much food that they could not survive.

 It goes on to describe the Kraken's feeding habits, claiming that it would trap the surrounding fish by stretching its neck with a belch releasing food from its mouth. The fish would be lured by the food and would enter the Kraken's mouth to feed. As a result, vast quantities of them would be trapped."

Recently, some huge squid have been discovered living in extraordinary depths and reaching about forty-five feet in length. The largest documented captured squid was by New Zealand vessel off the coast of Antarctica.

The beast weighed over a thousand pounds and was in excess of thirty-three feet in length.

It would have taken the world's biggest pot to cook it.

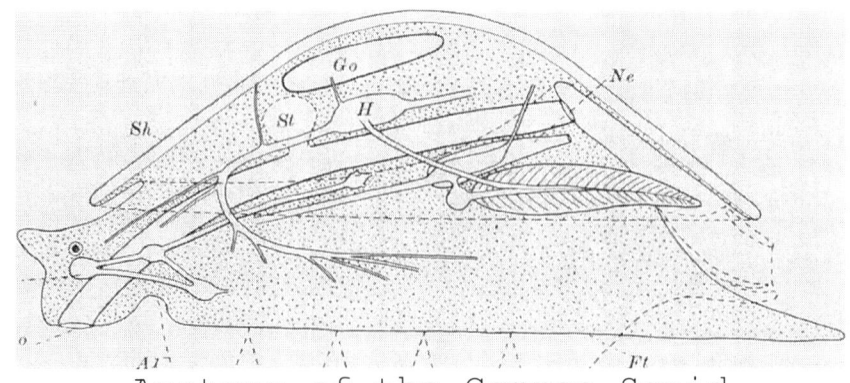

Anatomy of the Common Squid

2. CLEANING YOUR SQUID

Often squid will be purchased fully cleaned or even cut up into convenient shapes and sizes. However, sometimes the hardy cook will need to clean naughty squid so here is how to do it without losing a finger or an entire limb. This should not take more than a few minutes, more if you drink a whole bunch of beers while doing it. I recommend a pair of gloves since squiddy fingers can be misinterpreted.

Often cooks can be a bit squeamish over cleaning food, comparatively few will pluck and butcher a chicken, descale, clean and fillet a fish and squid are no different.

Sadly, there has always been an horrific connection between the seafood industry and child labor, particularly in the far east. It was reported "Thailand is the third largest seafood exporter in the world. The sector was worth some $7.3 billion dollars, and around a fifth of the catch ends up on American dinner tables — particularly tuna, sardines, shrimp and **squid.** But the industry heavily relies on trafficked and forced labor on unlicensed vessels. Victims typically hail from Cambodia, Laos and, most commonly, Burma. Beatings and starvation are commonplace." The following is a method I acquired from an old-timer who had spent many years as a squid cleaner and noted alcoholic in California, where fleets still catch squid of which Loligo is a local favorite.

Easy Cleaning Method

*Put on your protective gloves and drink a large gin and tonic.

*Holding the squiddy body nice and firmly, grasp the head and pull gently, twisting if necessary, to pull the head away from the body taking care not to rupture the naughty ink sac. If it does rupture you can rinse the ink away under cold water (see *post*) The internal body parts and tasty tentacles should easily come away with it.

*Cut the tentacles from the head just below the eyes. At the center of the tentacles is a nasty little small beak. Squeeze to remove the horrid thing and discard it or frighted a naughty child with it.
*Drink another gin and tonic
*Set aside the the tentacles to use later (they're edible and jolly tasty – see recipes *post*). If the recipe calls for ink (see post), reserve the ink, but if not discard the head together with the ink sac.
*At the top of the body, there is a

slim but clear piece of cartilage.
Pull it out of the body and discard
it.

*If the squid has an outer, somewhat
unattractive and slimy spotted skin,
carefully pull it off and discard it.

*Under cold running water, wash the
tube carefully, inside and out, to
remove any sand or residual tissue
bits and bobs tissues.

*Wash the tentacles very carefully and
reserve.

*If you're going to stuff the squidly
body tube (see recipes *post*), Set them
aside to drain.

*If you wish to fry them, remove the
side fins and reserve with the
tentacles for cooking since they're
equally edible. Finally let the lovely
creature strain and you are ready to
cook them Bon Appetit!

3. SQUID IN POPULAR CULTURE

Twenty Thousand Leagues Under the Sea
with a crew member providing a quick
snack for a giant squid

In many books and comics, movies,
television dramas, cartoons and music
many squiddy characters and references
appear. For example:

*In *The Deep Range* a massive squid is
captured and exhibited. In the short
story *Big Game Hunt*, a device capable
of controlling the behavior of
invertebrates is used in an attempt to
capture and film a giant squid. In
Washington these are called spokesmen.

*In *Animorphs* a series by K. A.
Applegate series a couple morph sperm
whales to find a giant squid, and then
the rest of the group morphs the one
squid to find the Pemalite ship.
*007 fights a giant squid in Ian
Fleming's *Dr. No*

Arthur C. Clarke frequently uses
squid in many of his works.

*H.P. Lovecraft frequently used tentacled, squid-like monsters in his novels.

*In *Moby Dick* Herman "Knuckles" Melville details the Pequods's slippery encounter with a giant squid. In *Childhood's End* one of the characters stows away on an alien spacecraft by hiding inside a model of a massive squid battling a whale.

*A giant squid also dwells, in an unlikely manner, in the lake at Hogwart's School in Rowling's awful *Harry Potter* series of books. It seems to be quite friendly towards the students.

*A giant squid acts as a minor character in Sheffield's novel *The Web Between the Worlds*.

*In Tolkien's Lord *of the Rings* a monster lurks in the waters of the Sirranon. Although Tolkien's description is not eltirely clear, the creature is frequently depicted as a giant squid.

*In Verne's classic *Twenty Thousand Leagues Under the Sea* the iconic Nautilus squabbles with seven giant squid.

*In Wyndham's *The Kraken Wakes* squiddy aliens invade earth

*In H. G. Wells' *The Sea Raiders* a peckish swarm of giant squids kill eleven people in boats.

*Peter Benchley's novel *Beast* features a giant squid terrorizing Bermuda. Benchley describes the Beast as having clawlike teeth in the center

of its suckers a a very squiddish
image or a politician

There are numerous other squiddy
creatures in television dramas and
cartoons. The marvelous Squidward in
Sponge Bob Square Pants being the
author's favorite. And, of course,
there are always Giant Squid, a post-
metal band (whatever that is) ,
Deathcore's song *Here Comes the Kraken*
and Wizard Rock's *The Giant
Squidstravaganza*.

4. THE RECIPES

Preparing lunch on The Nautilus

I have spent many wonderful vacations
in Andalusia, Spain where baby squid
in a very light batter is a quite
rightly popular tapas (*puntillitas*) in

the many wonderful little restaurants that I have pluckily stumbled both into and out of. Also in the Cantabrian Bay of Santander deep fried tentacles and thin strips of squid (*rabas de mango*) are delightful, particularly when washed down with several glasses of excellent local cider.

I lived in Turkey for a couple of years, and enjoyed deep fried strips of squid (kalamar tava and tarator sosu) along the lovely southern coast of that country. Squid is excellent when accompanied by Şalgam or Şalgam Suyu otherwise "turnip juice" which is a popular beverage in the southern cities. Şalgam is made with the juice of red carrot pickles, salted, spiced, and flavoured with aromatic turnip (*çelem*) fermented in barrels with the addition of ground bulgur. {see

Pepperell, K. Tiptoe Through The
Turnips – History, Folklore and
Recipes (2017)}

The Greeks love their calamari too
and it is often stuffed and then
grilled or served lightly breaded with
a tzatziki dip made of salted strained
goat milk yoghurt mixed with
cucumbers, garlic, salt, olive oil and
lemon juice, with just a hint of dill
and mint. Several bottle of retsina
and a pile of old plates should also
be available. I enjoyed many fine
squid dishes in the Greek Islands as a
young rascal.

Squid or calamari is common in the
fish and chip shops of Australia, New
Zealand, and South Africa.

In Italy and Spain it is a common
ingredient in seafood soups, paella,

and risotto. I enjoyed stewed squid and stuffed squid in Portugal and quid stuffed with rice, capers, and garlic and herbs and slowly stewed in red wine as I was slowly stewing in red wine myself.

In the Phillipines squid is a common street food and often charcoal grilled and is lovely as *dobong pusit*, or squid in adobo sauce, along with the inkproducing a lovely tangy flavour particulary when accompanied by fresh chillies.

The Koreans adore squid too and will eat it fresh and almost still wriggling about. It is also delicious as a street food. Dried squid is commonly served with peanuts. Squid is also roasted and served with hot pepper paste or

spicy mayonnaise as a dip. Steamed
squid and boiled squid are
considered (quite rightly) great
delicacies.

Squid is both a street food and a
special delicacy in South East
asia, China, India, Sri Lanka,
Taiwan, Japan, Russia, and
Thailand.

Calamari only really became popular
in The United States as recently as
the 1970. It is now commonly available
usually horribly over-battered and
over-cooked.

1. Lady Estima Davenport's Portuguese Squid Stew

Her Ladyship spent several years in
neutral Portugal during WW II while

working as an operative with MI6. This old family recipe was given to her by a very elderly Portuguese squid fisherman whose life she saved by sinking a Nazi U-Boat with nothing more than a can opener and a rather attractive Victorian sterling silver jam spoon.

Ingredients

1 1/2 lb. Best fresh quid

1/4 cup flour

1/4 cup extra virgin olive oil

1/3 cup best salted butter

1 large yellow onion, carefully peeled & chopped

2 cloves fresh garlic, chopped

12 fresh parsley sprigs with stalks removed

1/2 cup chopped peeled tomatoes

1/3 tsp. black pepper

Pinch crushed red pepper

Pinch of nun -blessed salt

1 tsp. Freshly chopped basil

I tsp. Freshly chopped oregano

A few slithers of fresh ginger

A glass of inexpensive Tinto wine.

Method.

Carefully clean the naughty squid (see *ante*) and cut in 1 inch pieces. Sprinkle with all purpose flour. Combine the extra virgin olive oil and butter in a favorite pan and heat. Add the yellow onions and cook to medium brown. Add garlic, ginger, and parsley; stir. Add the cut quid, stir, cover and cook for about 20 minutes. Add the tomatoes, Tinto wine, black and red pepper, salt, basil and oregano.

Stir, cover and cook for about 45

minutes. Keep stirring from time to time. Drink a few glasses of wine while waiting.

Excellent served with rice or pasta and a bottle or two of your favorite Tinto plonk.

2. Uncle Luigi's Friend of Ours Calamares A La Romana)

Uncle Luigi was a rather mysterious old fellow who lived in a small white-washed house on the coast of Western Sardinia. He was a noted chef and his squid preparations were legendary. Groups of burly men in dark suits and wearing sunglasses were regular visitors but locals never inquired why. Capische.

Ingredients

6 squid - small to medium – well

cleaned

2 fresh brown local large eggs --
beaten

1/2 cup all - purpose lour

3/4 cup olive oil (Luigi's own
Olive Oil Company product is
probably the wisest)

1 pinch nun-blessed salt

Method

 Lock the door and close the
shutters. Carefully wash the and
rinse the cleaned squid; remove
its tentacles; dry thoroughly.
Cut the body of squid into equal
sized rings, kiss the rings, dip
them in all-purpose flour, then
in egg beaten with a pinch of the
nun-blessed salt. Fry rings in
<u>very hot</u> oil.

The calamari is done as soon as it is browned on all sides. Frying time should never be above about four minutes to prevent its overcooked.

Peek out of the shutters. If all clear, drink some wine with relief and enjoy the squid with a little fresh lemon. Take a small tribute over to Luigi.

3. Ilias the Tiny Greek's Aegean Stuffed Squid

Ilias the tiny Greek is a legend in the kitchen now that he has left his native Athens and is hiding out in the lurid green bean casserole belt of the Mid-Western United States for reasons best know to him and Immigration. His lamb, grouper, and steak dishes are all sublime.

He is fond of stuffing squid and this recipe is a most excellent one.

Ingredients

12 naughty squid tubes

4 ounces best feta cheese

1/2 cup finely-chopped fresh shrimp

1 teaspoon grated Mayer lemon zest

1 teaspoon dried oregano

Nun-Blessed Salt to taste

Freshly-ground black pepper to taste

2 quarts favorite vegetable oil

1/2 cup all-purpose flour

1/2 cup whole milk

1/2 cup freshly made breadcrumbs

Method

Check there are no immigration agents nearby. Lock the door. Drink a beer. Rinse the nicely cleaned squid tubes inside and out and pat them dry them on a paper towel. They may hum with pleasure at this point.

Crumble the best feta cheese into bowl and add the shrimp, Mayer lemon zest, oregano, salt and pepper. Stir to thoroughly combine these ingredients.

Loosely fill each squid tube with about 1 1/2 tablespoons of the lovely stuffing mixture. Seal the top of the squid tube together and skewer with a wooden tooth pick to carefully enclose the stuffing.

Heat about 2 inches of fresh oil to 375 degrees in a deep-fryer. Put the all-purpose flour in a dish and season with salt and pepper. Put the milk in a second dish and the breadcrumbs in a third.

Dust the stuffed squid with seasoned flour then dip them in the milk and finally coat them with breadcrumbs.

Shake off excess breadcrumbs and cook a few at a time in, until golden brown 2 minutes should do. Drain and serve. Sometimes I put a few halved cooked Russian fingerlings in at the end. Yummy!

Enjoy with at least two bottles of retsina.

3. Sir Bunty Frobisher's Braised Squid with Artichokes

Noted country squire, sportsman,

rake and alcoholic Sir Bunty Frobisher was given this recipe by fellow rascal Count Jean-Luc Ballons.

 The two would often mount ostriches and ride to hounds with them with little success and always a lot of bruising and chaffed groinage.

Ingredients

1 nice juicy Mayer lemon
4 large well-trimmed artichokes
3 tablespoons extra virgin olive oil
1 tablespoon finely minced garlic
2 chopped anchovy fillets
2 pounds cleaned squid cut into rings
Freshly ground black pepper
Chopped fresh parsley for garnish

Method

Cut the naughty Mayer lemon in half, squeeze the juice into a small bowl of water, and add the lemon halves. Cut the trimmed artichokes into 4 pieces each, and add them to the lemon water to soak. Drink a glass or two of vintage port.

Place a broad saucepan over medium heat and add 2 tablespoons of the oil and a few seconds later carefully add the garlic and anchovies.

Cook, stirring occasionally, until the anchovies go all mushy and the garlic begins to takes on some color (probably about four minutes). Add the naughty squid

and the artichokes, stir, cover
and turn the heat to a medium
setting.

Uncover and stir the mixture
every few minutes or so. Drink
several beers. When the squid and
artichokes begin to become
tender, after 15 or 20 minutes or
so, uncover and cook until most
of the liquid has evaporated and
the squid and artichokes are nice
and naughtily tender, about 10 to
15 minutes more should do the
trick. Season with pepper to
taste. Add a drizzle of olive oil
and garnish with the chopped
fresh parsley. You are ready to
go!

4. Janet Frobisher's Catalan Sauteed Calamari

Janet Frobisher from Woollard End, Suffolk, England is a well-known serial killer and baker of delightfully moist Victoria sponge cakes. While on the lam from Holloway Woman's Prison, having tunneled her way out with only a small sterling silver mustard spoon, Janet managed to kayak to Spain. While hiding out and working in the kitchen of Pablo's Andorran Cafe she learn this recipe. Janet's parents, Inky and Imogen Quill, were killed in a bizarre ballooning accident and her late husband Brian succumbed to a cobra bite in India in 1947. Janet is probably quite bonkers.

Ingredients

1 1/4 lb Calamari together with

some naughty but well-cleaned tentacles

3 tablespoon of virgin or slightly naughty olive oil

1 dry red chile crumbled

3 large white or yellow Onions

Nun-blessed salt & white pepper to taste

Method

 Clean calamari (squid) and cut the across the tubes into 1/2" rings. Pat dry and set aside. In a medium skillet, heat one tablespoon of the oil over medium heat. Add the calamari and saute until they turn opaque white, probably forty-five seconds is enough. Set aside. Wipe skillet dry, add remaining oil and heat. Add chile and heat until it turns a darkish color. Remove chile and discard. Add the onions to the hot chile oil and cook for about 5 minutes. Stir and take care not to burn. Drink a beer or a glass of white wine. Reduce heat and cook onions slowly to caramelize 35 minutes should do the trick nicely. Keep stirring to prevent sticking. Drink another beer. Season to taste. Add calamari and stir until heated throughout.

Best served with nicely toasted and buttered French stick. Drink a bottle of dry white wine too.

5. Hirohito Fong's Squid and Tuna Sashimi

In the delifghtful Suffolk, England village of Woollard End, England local eccentric Millie Horseposture, had attempted to run Millie's Biscotti there for several years.

Sadly the recipe for the twice baked cantuccini biscuits handed down from her Italian grandmother Maria Spumanti of Prato had been woefully mistranslated. The resultant cookies were as a hard as a rock and entirely inedible. Many chipped and broken teeth (not uncommon among the English) provided painful testament to this. However, when the very large ones had been baked enterprising locals would turn them into useful domestic objects like door stops, roofing tiles,and knife grinders. Quite by chance, a Japanese visitor Hirohito Fong realised the industrial possibilities of Millie's indestructible product and acquired

the recipe for a very reasonable sum.
Mr. Fong's newly acquired biscotti
recipe had recently been utilized for
making the construction material
'Fongite'.

The imposing 1,245 feet tall Fong
Tower in Fukuoka on the northern
shore of the island of Kyushu is
constructed entirely from it. It is
claimed that Fongite can withstand an
earthquake and a major nuclear
attack.

 Fong's mother Elvira 'Chop-Chop'
Fong handed down to young Hirohito
the following family squid recipe.

Ingredients

2 raw cleaned squid
14 oz. raw Ahi tuna (nicely cut

into fillets)

Grated fresh horseradish for garnish

Favorite soy sauce

1 large sheet of dried seaweed

Method

Carefully cut the tuna into 1/2 inch squares using a sharp knife or a Samurai sword.

Remove the legs and the naughty top fin of the squid and remove the skin. Make slits on the quid surface 1/5 inch apart lengthwise. Don't cut it all the way through. Affix a sheet of seaweed to the bottom and roll squid, then cut.

Place ahi tuna and squid on a nice serving plate.

Garnish with a little grated
horseradish. Dip sashimi in the
soy sauce and gobble it down
noisily.

6. Socrates' Fried Squid

"Said Aristotle unto Plato,
'Have another sweet potato?'
Said Plato unto Aristotle,
'Thank you, I prefer the
bottle!"

{Owen Wister (1860-1938)
novelist}

Dear old Socrates (469-399 B.C.)
grew up during the golden age of
Pericles' Athens and is perhaps
best known as a questioner of
everything culinary and everyone

in the food industry. His style of cooking—immortalized as the Socratic Method—involved asking questions as to how his interlocutors wanted their squid and other delights cooked. After clarifying a recipe his diners eventually arrived at their own dishes. He was accused of corrupting the youth of Athens with a taramasalata recipe and sentenced to death. Choosing not to flee, he spent his final days in the company of his friends before drinking a poorly made lentil soup. This recipe (with some modern adaptions) derives from Plato's dialogue *A Taste of Clitophon*.

Ingredients

2 lb. whole fresh quid

2 tablespoon Mayer lemon juice

1 tablespoon nun-blessed salt

1/8 teaspoon ground white pepper

1 local large free-range brown egg
well beaten

2 tablespoons whole fresh milk

1 cup all-purpose flour

Favorite oil for frying

Method

Cut squid into several pieces. Cut
the tentacles into pieces about an
inch long. Drink a glass of ouzo. Ask
locals difficult questions. Drizzle
with Mayer lemon juice juice and
season to taste with nun-blessed salt
and ground white pepper. Ask
Xanthippe to get out of the kitchen.

Mix the whole milk and beaten egg
together in a bowl. Dip pieces of

squid in the mixture then roll in flour. Place in a single layer in hot oil using a medium sized skillet.

Fry one side at about 350F for four minutes or so. Repeat on the other side until both are lightly browned (another four minutes should do the trick) Drain and serve with lemon wedges and at least one bottle of Retsina. Don't invited Callicles over. Bon appetit!

7. Che Guevara's Squid with Revolutionary Mango, Mint and Chilli Salsa

Lady Estima Davenport and her old school chum and tennis partner Muriel Dinwiddy met Che Guevara in 1950 by the side of the road while they were enjoying was on a bicycling holiday in Northern Argentina

 Che had got a puncture and Lady Davenport masterfully repaired it for him using part of her Acme Rubberized Gentlewoman Bicyclist's Saddle Cozy.

 While the repairs were being completed Guevara made a great dish of his favorite quid that he shared with his traveling companion and the redoubtable ladies.

Ingredients

Twelve ounces of fresh medium sized revolution inclined squid
One pound of nice fresh rocket
2 Limes nicely juice
1 local ripe mango
1/4 small red (of course) onion

1/2 red (of course) chilli

Garlic

Fresh mint sprigs with stalks removed

Balsamic vinegar

Seasonings to taste

Method

 Carefully clean and remove the centers of the squid and neatly cut and trim into pieces. Char grill on a griddle pan and season with lime, chilli, garlic and pepper.

 Skin the mango, keeping as much flesh as you can.

 Finely chop the chilli, onion and mango combine in a bowl. Add some chopped mint, lime juice and some lime zest and to.

Dress the rocket and place onto the plate with the salsa and squid. Luverly!

8. Benito Mussolini's Traditional Squid and Seafood Fettuccine Duce

Lady Joan Pepperell, the author's mother met Mussolini at a social event when she was Cultural Attache to the British Embassy in 1925, two years after he had become Prime Minister of Italy (at the invitation of noted cross-dresser King Victor Emmanuel III).

She recalled he had been editor of the newspaper *Il Popolo d'Italia* and had written some excellent recipes in his column *Cook Today, Il Duce Tomorrow.*

Lady Joan referred to him as "a rum

looking cove with shifty eyes and troubled by hot searing wind. He had unseemly wandering hands to boot". Mussolini had brough some of his fettuccine to the event and it had been a big hit or so he announced.

He wrote the recipe down on a napkin and gave it to Lady Joan and it is faithfully set out overleaf.

Ingredients

1 small yellow onion finely chopped
1 clove worth of minced garlic,
1 tablespoon Italian olive oil
1 can tomato paste
1 can mushrooms (times were austere)
1 can crushed tomatoes
1/2 lb. fresh squid, cleaned and sliced
1/2 lb. bay scallops

1 lb. medium fresh cleaned a shrimp

1 lb. uncooked fettuccine

A lot of chopped fresh basil with stems removed

A bottle of wine for guzzling while you cook

Method

Brown the chopped garlic and onion in oil. Add the tomato paste and 1 can of water, paste can to measure. Cover and let cook 15 minutes. Add crushed tomatoes, mushrooms, and 1/2 cup water. Cook on a low heat for about for 30 minutes.

In a skillet cook the squid lightly dusted in some flour for about three minutes a side and reserve. Clean the skillet and cook shrimp and scallops until almost done. Reserve

Prepare your fettuccine and cook for about ten minutes. Al dente is for pussies!

Stir some of the sauce into the drained fettuccine and stir gently.

Stir the reserved seafood mixture into the remaining sauce and make sure it is all nice and warm.

Place in a nice naughty pile on the fettuccine.

Drink several bottles of Chianti.

9. The Venerable Japendra's Theravadin Squid with Lemongrass and Coconut

Some Theravadin Buddhist monks differ from other sects since they do not believe vegetarianism is necessary for followers of the Buddha. Vegetarianism was not a part of the early Buddhist tradition and the Buddha himself was not a vegetarian. The Buddha was fond of pizza and regularly enjoyed "one with everything".

The Buddha got his food either by collecting alms or by being invited to the houses of followers where, in both cases, he ate what he was given.

Before his enlightenment he had experimented with various diets eventually abandoning them believing that they did not contribute to spiritual development.

The *Nipata Sutta* advises immorality that makes one impure (morally and spiritually), not the eating of meat. The Buddha is often described as eating meat, he recommended meat broth as a cure for certain types of illness and was fond of quid it seems. However, some Buddhists gradually came to avoid meat eating.

  The Venerable Japendra was the leader of a small group of Theravadin squid eaters. This recipe appears in Atthaka Vagga, the President endorsed part of the Nipata Sutta.

Ingredients

8 oz freshly donated squid

1/2 stalk borrowed lemongrass

1/4 can alms coconut milk

1 tablespoon follower presented fish sauce

1 tablespoon loaned oil

1 found chilli nicely chopped

Method

Wash the squid and slice horizontally into nice rings. Heat the oil and fry the lemongrass, squid and fish sauce. Add the coconut milk and chilli. Serve in a small bowl in your hut on the side of a Himalayan peak.

10. Grandma Dolores Fatty Dubois' Squid Jambalaya

Noted Louisiana alligator wrestler and fabled jambalaya cook Dolores 'Fatty' Dubois obtained this recipe following a lengthy fist fight with Jean-Luc 'Frenchy' Dubonnet, a paddle boat captain and noted cross-dresser.

Frenchy always celebrated the latest Parisian modes by showing a finely turned calf and an alluring flicker of a favorite sequined ostrich feather fan.

Ingredients

2 lb. whole fresh squid frozen

1 qt. boiling water

1 tablespoon nun-blessed salt

1 cup sliced white onion

3/4 cup diced green pepper

1 clove garlic, minced

1/2 teaspoon thyme

1/4 teaspoon hot sauce

1/4 teaspoon white pepper

1 cup long grain rice

1/2 teaspoon paprika

1/2 teaspoon salt

1/4 cup melted butter

1/2 cup cheap dry white wine

1 large can tomatoes

Method

Cut squid mantle and tentacles into 1-inch pieces and carefully place in boiling salted water. Cover and simmer for 15 minutes or until squid are tender. Drain and rinse away. Cook the white onion, green pepper, and garlic in butter until tender. Add wine (drink the rest of the bottle immediately), tomatoes, and seasonings. Heat and mix thoroughly. Add the rice giving it all a right good stirring. Cover and simmer for approximately half an hour or until rice is done.

11. Sum Hung Dong's Poached Squid Soup

Noted Shanghai floating restaurant owner and felon Uncle Sum Dong developed this dish from ingredients suggested by his mother-in-law Mrs. Fang Fang. It is a great favorite among junk crews, kidnappers, and local pirates. The family poem is:

立显荣朝士, Stand tall & display unstintingly squid before gentlemen,

文方运际祥。And study & method will expand the borders of our fortune and our squid.

祖恩贻泽远, Ancestral favors bequeath kindness and squid through the ages,

世代永承昌。Descendants forever obliged for their prosperity and squid.

Ingredients

2 pound Squid

1 quart Fish stock

2 green onions chopped

2 tablespoon butter

1 tablespoon *Tamarin* sauce

Rice Balls

1 cup uncooked short grained rice

2 cup water with some sesame seeds

Method

Clean your fresh squid and set tentacles aside. Wash squid and cut into 1/2 inch slices. In a large saucepan, bring stock to a boil; put in cut quid and simmer for about 25 minutes. Prepare to fight off pirates. Drink some rice wine. Set free some child labor. Add green onions, butter, and tamarind, stirring until butter is melted. Serve with rice balls.

Rice Balls:

In a saucepan, bring rice and water to a boil. Reduce heat and cook rice, covered, until tender and quite sticky. Remove cover and cook. When rice is cool enough to handle, wet your hands and form rice balls 1-1/2 inches in diameter. Spread sesame seeds on a piece of wax paper and roll rice balls in them. This should produce about a dozen balls.

Little is known of the author now he is in a witness protection program save he is hiding out somewhere in the Mid-West green bean casserole belt.

Printed in Great Britain
by Amazon